This book belongs to:

_____

How to use this Prayer Journal

This is a 60-day prayer journal and can be utilized to explore God's word surrounding different aspects of your life.

How to enjoy the book, Step by Step:

- You will find a list of subjects and corresponding Bible verses on the next page (page 3).

- Each day, select a verse.

- Place a check mark in the circle next to the verse you select indicating that you have completed your studies of the verse

- You will find a space at the top of each day's page to write in the verse that you selected for that day.

- Follow the prompts provided.

EQUALITY

- ○ John 13:16
- ○ John 13:34
- ○ Proverbs 22:2
- ○ Romans 2:11
- ○ Acts 10:34-35
- ○ Galatians 3:28
- ○ Mark 12:31

ABUSE

- ○ Colossians 3:19
- ○ Proverbs 15:1
- ○ Ephesians 4:31
- ○ Psalm 9:9
- ○ Psalm 72:14
- ○ Psalm 147:3
- ○ Psalm 103:6

HEALTH

- ○ Proverbs 17:22
- ○ Jeremiah 33:6
- ○ Proverbs 16:24
- ○ Proverbs 3:7-8
- ○ Jeremiah 17:14
- ○ Exodus 23:25
- ○ Isaiah 41:10

STRENGTH

- ○ Philippians 4:13
- ○ Isaiah 40:29
- ○ Psalm 119:28
- ○ Ephesians 6:10
- ○ Isaiah 40:31
- ○ Psalm 46:1
- ○ Isaiah 41:10

FINANCES

- ○ Hebrews 13:5
- ○ Matthew 6:21
- ○ Psalm 37:16-17
- ○ Proverbs 13:11
- ○ Matthew 19:21
- ○ Matthew 6:24
- ○ 1 Timothy 6:10

STRUGGLES

- ○ Isaiah 41:13
- ○ 1 Peter 5:7
- ○ James 1:2-4
- ○ Proverbs 3:5-6
- ○ Proverbs 12:25
- ○ Romans 8:28
- ○ James 1:12

PROTECTION

- ○ Psalm 138:7
- ○ Deuteronomy 31:6
- ○ Psalm 20:1
- ○ Psalm 34:19
- ○ Psalm 51:1
- ○ Psalm 140:4

EDUCATION

- ○ Proverbs 2:1-2
- ○ Proverbs 20:15
- ○ Psalm 119:66
- ○ Proverbs 18:15
- ○ Proverbs 22:6
- ○ Proverbs 9:9

BEING THANKFUL

- ○ 1 Chronicles 16:34
- ○ Colossians 3:17
- ○ Colossians 4:2
- ○ Philippians 4:6
- ○ Psalm 28:7
- ○ Psalm 106:1

Today's Date:_____

Let God speak to you through his Word. Select a scripture from Page 3.

Scripture selected:_____

Write down the scripture:

Study the scripture, then pray and answer the following.

Write down how you're feeling about the topic of the scripture:

_____

_____

_____

_____

What's your prayer to God surrounding the scripture?

_____

_____

_____

_____

Other Prayer Requests:

_____   _____

_____   _____

_____   _____

_____   _____

Answered Prayer Requests:

_____   _____

_____   _____

_____   _____

_____   _____

Today I am most thankful for:

_____

_____

_____

_____

Today's Date:_____

Let God speak to you through his Word. Select a scripture from Page 3.

Scripture selected:_____

Write down the scripture:

Study the scripture, then pray and answer the following.

Write down how you're feeling about the topic of the scripture:

_____

_____

_____

_____

What's your prayer to God surrounding the scripture?

_____

_____

_____

_____

Other Prayer Requests:

_____   _____

_____   _____

_____   _____

_____   _____

Answered Prayer Requests:

_____   _____

_____   _____

_____   _____

_____   _____

Today I am most thankful for:

_____

_____

_____

_____

Today's Date:_____

Let God speak to you through his Word. Select a scripture from Page 3.

Scripture selected:_____

Write down the scripture:

Study the scripture, then pray and answer the following.

Write down how you're feeling about the topic of the scripture:

_____

_____

_____

_____

What's your prayer to God surrounding the scripture?

_____

_____

_____

_____

Other Prayer Requests:

_____   _____

_____   _____

_____   _____

_____   _____

Answered Prayer Requests:

_____   _____

_____   _____

_____   _____

_____   _____

Today I am most thankful for:

_____

_____

_____

_____

Today's Date:_____

Let God speak to you through his Word. Select a scripture from Page 3.

Scripture selected:_____

Write down the scripture:

Study the scripture, then pray and answer the following.

Write down how you're feeling about the topic of the scripture:

_____

_____

_____

_____

What's your prayer to God surrounding the scripture?

_____

_____

_____

_____

Other Prayer Requests:

_____ _____

_____ _____

_____ _____

_____ _____

Answered Prayer Requests:

_____ _____

_____ _____

_____ _____

_____ _____

Today I am most thankful for:

_____

_____

_____

_____

Today's Date:_____

Let God speak to you through his Word. Select a scripture from Page 3.

Scripture selected:_____

Write down the scripture:

Study the scripture, then pray and answer the following.

⌁ ⌁ ⌁ ⌁ ⌁ ⌁ ⌁ ⌁ ⌁

Write down how you're feeling about the topic of the scripture:

_____

_____

_____

_____

⌁ ⌁ ⌁ ⌁ ⌁ ⌁ ⌁ ⌁ ⌁

What's your prayer to God surrounding the scripture?

_____

_____

_____

_____

Other Prayer Requests:

_____   _____

_____   _____

_____   _____

_____   _____

Answered Prayer Requests:

_____   _____

_____   _____

_____   _____

_____   _____

Today I am most thankful for:

_____

_____

_____

_____

Today's Date:_____

Let God speak to you through his Word. Select a scripture from Page 3.

Scripture selected:_____

Write down the scripture:

Study the scripture, then pray and answer the following.

Write down how you're feeling about the topic of the scripture:

_____

_____

_____

_____

What's your prayer to God surrounding the scripture?

_____

_____

_____

_____

Other Prayer Requests:

_____   _____

_____   _____

_____   _____

_____   _____

Answered Prayer Requests:

_____   _____

_____   _____

_____   _____

_____   _____

Today I am most thankful for:

_____

_____

_____

_____

Today's Date:_____

Let God speak to you through his Word. Select a scripture from Page 3.

Scripture selected:_____

Write down the scripture:

Study the scripture, then pray and answer the following.

Write down how you're feeling about the topic of the scripture:

_____

_____

_____

_____

What's your prayer to God surrounding the scripture?

_____

_____

_____

_____

Other Prayer Requests:

_____   _____

_____   _____

_____   _____

_____   _____

Answered Prayer Requests:

_____   _____

_____   _____

_____   _____

_____   _____

Today I am most thankful for:

_____

_____

_____

_____

Today's Date:_____

Let God speak to you through his Word. Select a scripture from Page 3.

Scripture selected:_____

Write down the scripture:

Study the scripture, then pray and answer the following.

Write down how you're feeling about the topic of the scripture:

_____

_____

_____

_____

What's your prayer to God surrounding the scripture?

_____

_____

_____

_____

Other Prayer Requests:

_____   _____

_____   _____

_____   _____

_____   _____

Answered Prayer Requests:

_____   _____

_____   _____

_____   _____

_____   _____

Today I am most thankful for:

_____

_____

_____

_____

Today's Date:_____

Let God speak to you through his Word. Select a scripture from Page 3.

Scripture selected:_____

Write down the scripture:

Study the scripture, then pray and answer the following.

Write down how you're feeling about the topic of the scripture:

_____

_____

_____

_____

What's your prayer to God surrounding the scripture?

_____

_____

_____

_____

Other Prayer Requests:

_____   _____

_____   _____

_____   _____

_____   _____

Answered Prayer Requests:

_____   _____

_____   _____

_____   _____

_____   _____

Today I am most thankful for:

_____

_____

_____

_____

Today's Date:_____

Let God speak to you through his Word. Select a scripture from Page 3.

Scripture selected:_____

Write down the scripture:

Study the scripture, then pray and answer the following.

Write down how you're feeling about the topic of the scripture:

_____

_____

_____

_____

What's your prayer to God surrounding the scripture?

_____

_____

_____

_____

Other Prayer Requests:

_____   _____

_____   _____

_____   _____

_____   _____

Answered Prayer Requests:

_____   _____

_____   _____

_____   _____

_____   _____

Today I am most thankful for:

_____

_____

_____

_____

Today's Date:_____

Let God speak to you through his Word. Select a scripture from Page 3.

Scripture selected:_____

Write down the scripture:

Study the scripture, then pray and answer the following.

Write down how you're feeling about the topic of the scripture:

_____

_____

_____

_____

What's your prayer to God surrounding the scripture?

_____

_____

_____

_____

Other Prayer Requests:

_____   _____

_____   _____

_____   _____

_____   _____

Answered Prayer Requests:

_____   _____

_____   _____

_____   _____

_____   _____

Today I am most thankful for:

_____

_____

_____

_____

Today's Date:_____

Let God speak to you through his Word. Select a scripture from Page 3.

Scripture selected:_____

Write down the scripture:

Study the scripture, then pray and answer the following.

Write down how you're feeling about the topic of the scripture:

_____

_____

_____

_____

What's your prayer to God surrounding the scripture?

_____

_____

_____

_____

Other Prayer Requests:

_____ _____

_____ _____

_____ _____

_____ _____

Answered Prayer Requests:

_____ _____

_____ _____

_____ _____

_____ _____

Today I am most thankful for:

_____

_____

_____

_____

Today's Date:_____

Let God speak to you through his Word. Select a scripture from Page 3.

Scripture selected:_____

Write down the scripture:

Study the scripture, then pray and answer the following.

Write down how you're feeling about the topic of the scripture:

_____

_____

_____

_____

What's your prayer to God surrounding the scripture?

_____

_____

_____

_____

Other Prayer Requests:

_____   _____

_____   _____

_____   _____

_____   _____

Answered Prayer Requests:

_____   _____

_____   _____

_____   _____

_____   _____

Today I am most thankful for:

_____

_____

_____

_____

Today's Date:_____

Let God speak to you through his Word. Select a scripture from Page 3.

Scripture selected:_____

Write down the scripture:

Study the scripture, then pray and answer the following.

Write down how you're feeling about the topic of the scripture:

_____

_____

_____

_____

What's your prayer to God surrounding the scripture?

_____

_____

_____

_____

Other Prayer Requests:

_____   _____

_____   _____

_____   _____

_____   _____

Answered Prayer Requests:

_____   _____

_____   _____

_____   _____

_____   _____

Today I am most thankful for:

_____

_____

_____

_____

Today's Date:_____

Let God speak to you through his Word. Select a scripture from Page 3.

Scripture selected:_____

Write down the scripture:

Study the scripture, then pray and answer the following.

Write down how you're feeling about the topic of the scripture:

_____

_____

_____

_____

What's your prayer to God surrounding the scripture?

_____

_____

_____

_____

Other Prayer Requests:

_____   _____

_____   _____

_____   _____

_____   _____

Answered Prayer Requests:

_____   _____

_____   _____

_____   _____

_____   _____

Today I am most thankful for:

_____

_____

_____

_____

Today's Date:_____

Let God speak to you through his Word. Select a scripture from Page 3.

Scripture selected:_____

Write down the scripture:

Study the scripture, then pray and answer the following.

Write down how you're feeling about the topic of the scripture:

_____

_____

_____

_____

What's your prayer to God surrounding the scripture?

_____

_____

_____

_____

Other Prayer Requests:

_____   _____

_____   _____

_____   _____

_____   _____

Answered Prayer Requests:

_____   _____

_____   _____

_____   _____

_____   _____

Today I am most thankful for:

_____

_____

_____

_____

Today's Date:_____

Let God speak to you through his Word. Select a scripture from Page 3.

Scripture selected:_____

Write down the scripture:

Study the scripture, then pray and answer the following.

Write down how you're feeling about the topic of the scripture:

_____

_____

_____

_____

What's your prayer to God surrounding the scripture?

_____

_____

_____

_____

Other Prayer Requests:

_____   _____

_____   _____

_____   _____

_____   _____

Answered Prayer Requests:

_____   _____

_____   _____

_____   _____

_____   _____

Today I am most thankful for:

_____

_____

_____

_____

Today's Date:_____

Let God speak to you through his Word. Select a scripture from Page 3.

Scripture selected:_____

Write down the scripture:

Study the scripture, then pray and answer the following.

Write down how you're feeling about the topic of the scripture:

_____

_____

_____

_____

What's your prayer to God surrounding the scripture?

_____

_____

_____

_____

Other Prayer Requests:

_____   _____

_____   _____

_____   _____

_____   _____

Answered Prayer Requests:

_____   _____

_____   _____

_____   _____

_____   _____

Today I am most thankful for:

_____

_____

_____

_____

Today's Date:_____

Let God speak to you through his Word. Select a scripture from Page 3.

Scripture selected:_____

Write down the scripture:

Study the scripture, then pray and answer the following.

Write down how you're feeling about the topic of the scripture:

_____

_____

_____

_____

What's your prayer to God surrounding the scripture?

_____

_____

_____

_____

Other Prayer Requests:

_____   _____

_____   _____

_____   _____

_____   _____

Answered Prayer Requests:

_____   _____

_____   _____

_____   _____

_____   _____

Today I am most thankful for:

_____

_____

_____

_____

Today's Date:_____

Let God speak to you through his Word. Select a scripture from Page 3.

Scripture selected:_____

Write down the scripture:

Study the scripture, then pray and answer the following.

Write down how you're feeling about the topic of the scripture:

_____

_____

_____

_____

What's your prayer to God surrounding the scripture?

_____

_____

_____

_____

Other Prayer Requests:

_____   _____

_____   _____

_____   _____

_____   _____

Answered Prayer Requests:

_____   _____

_____   _____

_____   _____

_____   _____

Today I am most thankful for:

_____

_____

_____

_____

Today's Date:_____

Let God speak to you through his Word. Select a scripture from Page 3.

Scripture selected:_____

Write down the scripture:

Study the scripture, then pray and answer the following.

Write down how you're feeling about the topic of the scripture:

_____

_____

_____

_____

What's your prayer to God surrounding the scripture?

_____

_____

_____

_____

Other Prayer Requests:

_____   _____

_____   _____

_____   _____

_____   _____

Answered Prayer Requests:

_____   _____

_____   _____

_____   _____

_____   _____

Today I am most thankful for:

_____

_____

_____

_____

Today's Date:_____

Let God speak to you through his Word. Select a scripture from Page 3.

Scripture selected:_____

Write down the scripture:

Study the scripture, then pray and answer the following.

Write down how you're feeling about the topic of the scripture:

_____

_____

_____

_____

What's your prayer to God surrounding the scripture?

_____

_____

_____

_____

Other Prayer Requests:

_____ _____

_____ _____

_____ _____

_____ _____

Answered Prayer Requests:

_____ _____

_____ _____

_____ _____

_____ _____

Today I am most thankful for:

_____

_____

_____

_____

Today's Date:_____

Let God speak to you through his Word. Select a scripture from Page 3.

Scripture selected:_____

Write down the scripture:

Study the scripture, then pray and answer the following.

Write down how you're feeling about the topic of the scripture:

_____

_____

_____

_____

What's your prayer to God surrounding the scripture?

_____

_____

_____

_____

Other Prayer Requests:

_____   _____

_____   _____

_____   _____

_____   _____

Answered Prayer Requests:

_____   _____

_____   _____

_____   _____

_____   _____

Today I am most thankful for:

_____

_____

_____

_____

Today's Date:_____

Let God speak to you through his Word. Select a scripture from Page 3.

Scripture selected:_____

Write down the scripture:

Study the scripture, then pray and answer the following.

Write down how you're feeling about the topic of the scripture:

_____

_____

_____

_____

What's your prayer to God surrounding the scripture?

_____

_____

_____

_____

Other Prayer Requests:

_____   _____

_____   _____

_____   _____

_____   _____

Answered Prayer Requests:

_____   _____

_____   _____

_____   _____

_____   _____

Today I am most thankful for:

_____

_____

_____

_____

Today's Date:_____

Let God speak to you through his Word. Select a scripture from Page 3.

Scripture selected:_____

Write down the scripture:

Study the scripture, then pray and answer the following.

Write down how you're feeling about the topic of the scripture:

_____

_____

_____

_____

What's your prayer to God surrounding the scripture?

_____

_____

_____

_____

Other Prayer Requests:

_____   _____

_____   _____

_____   _____

_____   _____

Answered Prayer Requests:

_____   _____

_____   _____

_____   _____

_____   _____

Today I am most thankful for:

_____

_____

_____

_____

Today's Date:_____

Let God speak to you through his Word. Select a scripture from Page 3.

Scripture selected:_____

Write down the scripture:

Study the scripture, then pray and answer the following.

Write down how you're feeling about the topic of the scripture:

_____

_____

_____

_____

What's your prayer to God surrounding the scripture?

_____

_____

_____

_____

Other Prayer Requests:

_____ _____

_____ _____

_____ _____

_____ _____

Answered Prayer Requests:

_____ _____

_____ _____

_____ _____

_____ _____

Today I am most thankful for:

_____

_____

_____

_____

Today's Date:_____

Let God speak to you through his Word. Select a scripture from Page 3.

Scripture selected:_____

Write down the scripture:

Study the scripture, then pray and answer the following.

Write down how you're feeling about the topic of the scripture:

_____

_____

_____

_____

What's your prayer to God surrounding the scripture?

_____

_____

_____

_____

Other Prayer Requests:

_____   _____

_____   _____

_____   _____

_____   _____

Answered Prayer Requests:

_____   _____

_____   _____

_____   _____

_____   _____

Today I am most thankful for:

_____

_____

_____

_____

Today's Date:_____

Let God speak to you through his Word. Select a scripture from Page 3.

Scripture selected:_____

Write down the scripture:

Study the scripture, then pray and answer the following.

Write down how you're feeling about the topic of the scripture:

_____

_____

_____

_____

What's your prayer to God surrounding the scripture?

_____

_____

_____

_____

Other Prayer Requests:

_____   _____

_____   _____

_____   _____

_____   _____

Answered Prayer Requests:

_____   _____

_____   _____

_____   _____

_____   _____

Today I am most thankful for:

_____

_____

_____

_____

Today's Date:_____

Let God speak to you through his Word. Select a scripture from Page 3.

Scripture selected:_____

Write down the scripture:

Study the scripture, then pray and answer the following.

Write down how you're feeling about the topic of the scripture:

_____

_____

_____

_____

What's your prayer to God surrounding the scripture?

_____

_____

_____

_____

Other Prayer Requests:

_____   _____

_____   _____

_____   _____

_____   _____

Answered Prayer Requests:

_____   _____

_____   _____

_____   _____

_____   _____

Today I am most thankful for:

_____

_____

_____

_____

Today's Date:_____

Let God speak to you through his Word. Select a scripture from Page 3.

Scripture selected:_____

Write down the scripture:

Study the scripture, then pray and answer the following.

Write down how you're feeling about the topic of the scripture:

_____

_____

_____

_____

What's your prayer to God surrounding the scripture?

_____

_____

_____

_____

Other Prayer Requests:

_____   _____

_____   _____

_____   _____

_____   _____

Answered Prayer Requests:

_____   _____

_____   _____

_____   _____

_____   _____

Today I am most thankful for:

_____

_____

_____

_____

Today's Date:_____

Let God speak to you through his Word. Select a scripture from Page 3.

Scripture selected:_____

Write down the scripture:

Study the scripture, then pray and answer the following.

Write down how you're feeling about the topic of the scripture:

_____

_____

_____

_____

What's your prayer to God surrounding the scripture?

_____

_____

_____

_____

Other Prayer Requests:

_____ _____

_____ _____

_____ _____

_____ _____

Answered Prayer Requests:

_____ _____

_____ _____

_____ _____

_____ _____

Today I am most thankful for:

_____

_____

_____

_____

Today's Date:_____

Let God speak to you through his Word. Select a scripture from Page 3.

Scripture selected:_____

Write down the scripture:

Study the scripture, then pray and answer the following.

Write down how you're feeling about the topic of the scripture:

_____

_____

_____

_____

What's your prayer to God surrounding the scripture?

_____

_____

_____

_____

Other Prayer Requests:

_____   _____

_____   _____

_____   _____

_____   _____

Answered Prayer Requests:

_____   _____

_____   _____

_____   _____

_____   _____

Today I am most thankful for:

_____

_____

_____

_____

Today's Date:_____

Let God speak to you through his Word. Select a scripture from Page 3.

Scripture selected:_____

Write down the scripture:

Study the scripture, then pray and answer the following.

Write down how you're feeling about the topic of the scripture:

_____

_____

_____

_____

What's your prayer to God surrounding the scripture?

_____

_____

_____

_____

Other Prayer Requests:

_____   _____

_____   _____

_____   _____

_____   _____

Answered Prayer Requests:

_____   _____

_____   _____

_____   _____

_____   _____

Today I am most thankful for:

_____

_____

_____

_____

Today's Date:_____

Let God speak to you through his Word. Select a scripture from Page 3.

Scripture selected:_____

Write down the scripture:

Study the scripture, then pray and answer the following.

❧ ・ ❧ ・ ❧ ・ ❧ ・

Write down how you're feeling about the topic of the scripture:

_____

_____

_____

_____

❧ ・ ❧ ・ ❧ ・ ❧ ・

What's your prayer to God surrounding the scripture?

_____

_____

_____

_____

Other Prayer Requests:

_____   _____

_____   _____

_____   _____

_____   _____

Answered Prayer Requests:

_____   _____

_____   _____

_____   _____

_____   _____

Today I am most thankful for:

_____

_____

_____

_____

Today's Date:_____

Let God speak to you through his Word. Select a scripture from Page 3.

Scripture selected:_____

Write down the scripture:

Study the scripture, then pray and answer the following.

Write down how you're feeling about the topic of the scripture:

_____

_____

_____

_____

What's your prayer to God surrounding the scripture?

_____

_____

_____

_____

Other Prayer Requests:

_____   _____

_____   _____

_____   _____

_____   _____

Answered Prayer Requests:

_____   _____

_____   _____

_____   _____

_____   _____

Today I am most thankful for:

_____

_____

_____

_____

Today's Date:_____

Let God speak to you through his Word. Select a scripture from Page 3.

Scripture selected:_____

Write down the scripture:

Study the scripture, then pray and answer the following.

Write down how you're feeling about the topic of the scripture:

_____

_____

_____

_____

What's your prayer to God surrounding the scripture?

_____

_____

_____

_____

Other Prayer Requests:

_____   _____

_____   _____

_____   _____

_____   _____

Answered Prayer Requests:

_____   _____

_____   _____

_____   _____

_____   _____

Today I am most thankful for:

_____

_____

_____

_____

Today's Date:_____

Let God speak to you through his Word. Select a scripture from Page 3.

Scripture selected:_____

Write down the scripture:

Study the scripture, then pray and answer the following.

Write down how you're feeling about the topic of the scripture:

_____

_____

_____

_____

What's your prayer to God surrounding the scripture?

_____

_____

_____

_____

Other Prayer Requests:

_____ _____

_____ _____

_____ _____

_____ _____

Answered Prayer Requests:

_____ _____

_____ _____

_____ _____

_____ _____

Today I am most thankful for:

_____

_____

_____

_____

Today's Date:_____

Let God speak to you through his Word. Select a scripture from Page 3.

Scripture selected:_____

Write down the scripture:

Study the scripture, then pray and answer the following.

Write down how you're feeling about the topic of the scripture:

_____

_____

_____

_____

What's your prayer to God surrounding the scripture?

_____

_____

_____

_____

Other Prayer Requests:

_____   _____

_____   _____

_____   _____

_____   _____

Answered Prayer Requests:

_____   _____

_____   _____

_____   _____

_____   _____

Today I am most thankful for:

_____

_____

_____

_____

Today's Date:_____

Let God speak to you through his Word. Select a scripture from Page 3.

Scripture selected:_____

Write down the scripture:

Study the scripture, then pray and answer the following.

Write down how you're feeling about the topic of the scripture:

_____

_____

_____

_____

What's your prayer to God surrounding the scripture?

_____

_____

_____

_____

Other Prayer Requests:

_____   _____

_____   _____

_____   _____

_____   _____

Answered Prayer Requests:

_____   _____

_____   _____

_____   _____

_____   _____

Today I am most thankful for:

_____

_____

_____

_____

Today's Date:_____

Let God speak to you through his Word. Select a scripture from Page 3.

Scripture selected:_____

Write down the scripture:

Study the scripture, then pray and answer the following.

Write down how you're feeling about the topic of the scripture:

_____

_____

_____

_____

What's your prayer to God surrounding the scripture?

_____

_____

_____

_____

Other Prayer Requests:

_____   _____

_____   _____

_____   _____

_____   _____

Answered Prayer Requests:

_____   _____

_____   _____

_____   _____

_____   _____

Today I am most thankful for:

_____

_____

_____

_____

Today's Date:_____

Let God speak to you through his Word. Select a scripture from Page 3.

Scripture selected:_____

Write down the scripture:

Study the scripture, then pray and answer the following.

Write down how you're feeling about the topic of the scripture:

_____

_____

_____

_____

What's your prayer to God surrounding the scripture?

_____

_____

_____

_____

Other Prayer Requests:

_____   _____

_____   _____

_____   _____

_____   _____

Answered Prayer Requests:

_____   _____

_____   _____

_____   _____

_____   _____

Today I am most thankful for:

_____

_____

_____

_____

Today's Date:_____

Let God speak to you through his Word. Select a scripture from Page 3.

Scripture selected:_____

Write down the scripture:

Study the scripture, then pray and answer the following.

Write down how you're feeling about the topic of the scripture:

_____

_____

_____

_____

What's your prayer to God surrounding the scripture?

_____

_____

_____

_____

Other Prayer Requests:

_____ _____

_____ _____

_____ _____

_____ _____

Answered Prayer Requests:

_____ _____

_____ _____

_____ _____

_____ _____

Today I am most thankful for:

_____

_____

_____

_____

Today's Date:_____

Let God speak to you through his Word. Select a scripture from Page 3.

Scripture selected:_____

Write down the scripture:

Study the scripture, then pray and answer the following.

Write down how you're feeling about the topic of the scripture:

_____

_____

_____

_____

What's your prayer to God surrounding the scripture?

_____

_____

_____

_____

Other Prayer Requests:

_____   _____

_____   _____

_____   _____

_____   _____

Answered Prayer Requests:

_____   _____

_____   _____

_____   _____

_____   _____

Today I am most thankful for:

_____

_____

_____

_____

Today's Date:_____

Let God speak to you through his Word. Select a scripture from Page 3.

Scripture selected:_____

Write down the scripture:

Study the scripture, then pray and answer the following.

Write down how you're feeling about the topic of the scripture:

_____

_____

_____

_____

What's your prayer to God surrounding the scripture?

_____

_____

_____

_____

Other Prayer Requests:

_____   _____

_____   _____

_____   _____

_____   _____

Answered Prayer Requests:

_____   _____

_____   _____

_____   _____

_____   _____

Today I am most thankful for:

_____

_____

_____

_____

Today's Date:_____

Let God speak to you through his Word. Select a scripture from Page 3.

Scripture selected:_____

Write down the scripture:

Study the scripture, then pray and answer the following.

Write down how you're feeling about the topic of the scripture:

_____

_____

_____

_____

What's your prayer to God surrounding the scripture?

_____

_____

_____

_____

Other Prayer Requests:

_____   _____

_____   _____

_____   _____

_____   _____

Answered Prayer Requests:

_____   _____

_____   _____

_____   _____

_____   _____

Today I am most thankful for:

_____

_____

_____

_____

Today's Date:_____

Let God speak to you through his Word. Select a scripture from Page 3.

Scripture selected:_____

Write down the scripture:

Study the scripture, then pray and answer the following.

Write down how you're feeling about the topic of the scripture:

_____

_____

_____

_____

What's your prayer to God surrounding the scripture?

_____

_____

_____

_____

Other Prayer Requests:

_____   _____

_____   _____

_____   _____

_____   _____

Answered Prayer Requests:

_____   _____

_____   _____

_____   _____

_____   _____

Today I am most thankful for:

_____

_____

_____

_____

Today's Date:_____

Let God speak to you through his Word. Select a scripture from Page 3.

Scripture selected:_____

Write down the scripture:

Study the scripture, then pray and answer the following.

Write down how you're feeling about the topic of the scripture:

_____

_____

_____

_____

What's your prayer to God surrounding the scripture?

_____

_____

_____

_____

Other Prayer Requests:

_____   _____

_____   _____

_____   _____

_____   _____

Answered Prayer Requests:

_____   _____

_____   _____

_____   _____

_____   _____

Today I am most thankful for:

_____

_____

_____

_____

Today's Date:_____

Let God speak to you through his Word. Select a scripture from Page 3.

Scripture selected:_____

Write down the scripture:

Study the scripture, then pray and answer the following.

Write down how you're feeling about the topic of the scripture:

_____

_____

_____

_____

What's your prayer to God surrounding the scripture?

_____

_____

_____

_____

Other Prayer Requests:

_____   _____

_____   _____

_____   _____

_____   _____

Answered Prayer Requests:

_____   _____

_____   _____

_____   _____

_____   _____

Today I am most thankful for:

_____

_____

_____

_____

Today's Date:_____

Let God speak to you through his Word. Select a scripture from Page 3.

Scripture selected:_____

Write down the scripture:

Study the scripture, then pray and answer the following.

Write down how you're feeling about the topic of the scripture:

_____

_____

_____

_____

What's your prayer to God surrounding the scripture?

_____

_____

_____

_____

Other Prayer Requests:

_____   _____

_____   _____

_____   _____

_____   _____

Answered Prayer Requests:

_____   _____

_____   _____

_____   _____

_____   _____

Today I am most thankful for:

_____

_____

_____

_____

Today's Date:_____

Let God speak to you through his Word. Select a scripture from Page 3.

Scripture selected:_____

Write down the scripture:

Study the scripture, then pray and answer the following.

⟨⟨⟨⟨⟨⟨⟨⟨⟨⟨⟨⟨⟨⟨⟨⟨⟨⟨⟨⟨⟩⟩

Write down how you're feeling about the topic of the scripture:

_____

_____

_____

_____

⟨⟨⟨⟨⟨⟨⟨⟨⟨⟨⟨⟨⟨⟨⟨⟨⟨⟨⟨⟨⟩⟩

What's your prayer to God surrounding the scripture?

_____

_____

_____

_____

Other Prayer Requests:

_____   _____

_____   _____

_____   _____

_____   _____

Answered Prayer Requests:

_____   _____

_____   _____

_____   _____

_____   _____

Today I am most thankful for:

_____

_____

_____

_____

Today's Date:_____

Let God speak to you through his Word. Select a scripture from Page 3.

Scripture selected:_____

Write down the scripture:

Study the scripture, then pray and answer the following.

Write down how you're feeling about the topic of the scripture:

_____

_____

_____

_____

What's your prayer to God surrounding the scripture?

_____

_____

_____

_____

Other Prayer Requests:

_____   _____

_____   _____

_____   _____

_____   _____

Answered Prayer Requests:

_____   _____

_____   _____

_____   _____

_____   _____

Today I am most thankful for:

_____

_____

_____

_____

Today's Date:_____

Let God speak to you through his Word. Select a scripture from Page 3.

Scripture selected:_____

Write down the scripture:

Study the scripture, then pray and answer the following.

Write down how you're feeling about the topic of the scripture:

_____

_____

_____

_____

What's your prayer to God surrounding the scripture?

_____

_____

_____

_____

Other Prayer Requests:

_____   _____

_____   _____

_____   _____

_____   _____

Answered Prayer Requests:

_____   _____

_____   _____

_____   _____

_____   _____

Today I am most thankful for:

_____

_____

_____

_____

Today's Date:_____

Let God speak to you through his Word. Select a scripture from Page 3.

Scripture selected:_____

Write down the scripture:

Study the scripture, then pray and answer the following.

Write down how you're feeling about the topic of the scripture:

_____

_____

_____

_____

What's your prayer to God surrounding the scripture?

_____

_____

_____

_____

Other Prayer Requests:

_____   _____

_____   _____

_____   _____

_____   _____

Answered Prayer Requests:

_____   _____

_____   _____

_____   _____

_____   _____

Today I am most thankful for:

_____

_____

_____

_____

Today's Date:_____

Let God speak to you through his Word. Select a scripture from Page 3.

Scripture selected:_____

Write down the scripture:

Study the scripture, then pray and answer the following.

Write down how you're feeling about the topic of the scripture:

_____

_____

_____

_____

What's your prayer to God surrounding the scripture?

_____

_____

_____

_____

Other Prayer Requests:

_____   _____

_____   _____

_____   _____

_____   _____

Answered Prayer Requests:

_____   _____

_____   _____

_____   _____

_____   _____

Today I am most thankful for:

_____

_____

_____

_____

Today's Date:_____

Let God speak to you through his Word. Select a scripture from Page 3.

Scripture selected:_____

Write down the scripture:

Study the scripture, then pray and answer the following.

Write down how you're feeling about the topic of the scripture:

_____

_____

_____

_____

What's your prayer to God surrounding the scripture?

_____

_____

_____

_____

Other Prayer Requests:

_____   _____

_____   _____

_____   _____

_____   _____

Answered Prayer Requests:

_____   _____

_____   _____

_____   _____

_____   _____

Today I am most thankful for:

_____

_____

_____

_____

Today's Date:_____

Let God speak to you through his Word. Select a scripture from Page 3.

Scripture selected:_____

Write down the scripture:

Study the scripture, then pray and answer the following.

Write down how you're feeling about the topic of the scripture:

_____
_____
_____
_____

What's your prayer to God surrounding the scripture?

_____
_____
_____
_____

Other Prayer Requests:

_____   _____

_____   _____

_____   _____

_____   _____

Answered Prayer Requests:

_____   _____

_____   _____

_____   _____

_____   _____

Today I am most thankful for:

_____

_____

_____

_____

Today's Date:_____

Let God speak to you through his Word. Select a scripture from Page 3.

Scripture selected:_____

Write down the scripture:

Study the scripture, then pray and answer the following.

Write down how you're feeling about the topic of the scripture:

_____

_____

_____

_____

What's your prayer to God surrounding the scripture?

_____

_____

_____

_____

Other Prayer Requests:

_____   _____

_____   _____

_____   _____

_____   _____

Answered Prayer Requests:

_____   _____

_____   _____

_____   _____

_____   _____

Today I am most thankful for:

_____

_____

_____

_____

Today's Date:_____

Let God speak to you through his Word. Select a scripture from Page 3.

Scripture selected:_____

Write down the scripture:

Study the scripture, then pray and answer the following.

Write down how you're feeling about the topic of the scripture:

_____

_____

_____

_____

What's your prayer to God surrounding the scripture?

_____

_____

_____

_____

Other Prayer Requests:

_____   _____

_____   _____

_____   _____

_____   _____

Answered Prayer Requests:

_____   _____

_____   _____

_____   _____

_____   _____

Today I am most thankful for:

_____

_____

_____

_____

Today's Date:_____

Let God speak to you through his Word. Select a scripture from Page 3.

Scripture selected:_____

Write down the scripture:

Study the scripture, then pray and answer the following.

Write down how you're feeling about the topic of the scripture:

_____

_____

_____

_____

What's your prayer to God surrounding the scripture?

_____

_____

_____

_____

Other Prayer Requests:

_____   _____

_____   _____

_____   _____

_____   _____

Answered Prayer Requests:

_____   _____

_____   _____

_____   _____

_____   _____

Today I am most thankful for:

_____

_____

_____

_____

Today's Date:_____

Let God speak to you through his Word. Select a scripture from Page 3.

Scripture selected:_____

Write down the scripture:

Study the scripture, then pray and answer the following.

Write down how you're feeling about the topic of the scripture:

_____

_____

_____

_____

What's your prayer to God surrounding the scripture?

_____

_____

_____

_____

Other Prayer Requests:

_____ _____

_____ _____

_____ _____

_____ _____

Answered Prayer Requests:

_____ _____

_____ _____

_____ _____

_____ _____

Today I am most thankful for:

_____

_____

_____

_____

Made in the USA
Coppell, TX
10 November 2020